contents

Honey and Spice Glazed Turkey

PREP 20 minutes   **COOK** 3 hours

HONEY AND SPICE GLAZE

- 2 tablespoons honey
- 2 teaspoons chili powder
- 1 teaspoon water
- ½ teaspoon garlic powder
- ¼ teaspoon ground allspice
- ¼ teaspoon ground cumin
- ¼ teaspoon salt
- ⅛ teaspoon ground red pepper

TURKEY

- 1 (14- to 16-pound) BUTTERBALL® Fresh or Frozen Whole Turkey, thawed if frozen

  Vegetable oil

1. Preheat oven to 325°F. Combine honey, chili powder, water, garlic powder, allspice, cumin, salt and red pepper in small bowl; mix well.

2. Remove neck and giblets from body and neck cavities of turkey. Refrigerate for another use or discard. Pat turkey dry with paper towels. Turn wings back to hold neck skin in place. Return legs to tucked position, if untucked. Place turkey, breast side up, on flat rack in shallow roasting pan. Brush with oil.

3. Roast turkey 1½ hours. Then, cover breast and top of drumsticks loosely with aluminum foil to prevent overcooking.

4. Continue roasting turkey 45 minutes to 1 hour. Uncover turkey breast and brush with honey-spice mixture. Cover breast with foil and continue roasting turkey 30 minutes to 1 hour* or until meat thermometer reaches 180°F when inserted into deepest part of thigh not touching bone.

5. Transfer turkey to cutting board; loosely tent with foil. Let stand 15 minutes before carving.

Follow cooking times according to package directions; times vary with size of turkey.

Makes 12 to 14 servings

the whole *turkey*

Roast Turkey with Pan Juices

PREP 20 minutes   **COOK** 3½ to 3¾ hours

1 (12- to 14-pound) BUTTERBALL®
   Fresh or Frozen Whole Turkey,
   thawed if frozen

1 Granny Smith apple, peeled and
   cut into 1-inch pieces

1 small onion, cut into quarters

2 carrots, cut into 1-inch pieces

2 stalks celery, cut into 1-inch
   pieces

5 sprigs fresh sage

5 sprigs fresh thyme
   Vegetable oil

3 cups fat-free chicken broth

1. Preheat oven to 325°F. Remove neck and giblets from body and neck cavities of turkey. Refrigerate for another use or discard. Pat turkey dry with paper towels. Turn wings back to hold neck skin in place. Place apple, onion, carrots, celery, sage and thyme in body cavity. Return legs to tucked position, if untucked. Place turkey, breast side up, on flat rack in shallow roasting pan. Brush breast and legs lightly with oil.

2. Roast turkey 1½ hours. Then, cover breast and top of drumsticks loosely with aluminum foil to prevent overcooking.

3. Continue roasting turkey 1½ to 2 hours* or until meat thermometer reaches 180°F when inserted into deepest part of thigh not touching bone.

4. Transfer turkey to cutting board. Transfer apple, vegetables and herbs from body cavity to roasting pan. Loosely tent turkey with foil while preparing pan juices.

5. Place roasting pan on burners over medium heat. Bring to a boil, stirring to scrape browned bits from bottom of pan. Stir in broth; bring to a boil. Reduce heat to medium-low; simmer 20 minutes, skimming excess fat from mixture. Remove from heat. Strain mixture through fine-mesh sieve before serving with turkey.

*Follow cooking times according to package directions; times vary with size of turkey.

Makes 10 to 12 servings

Roast Turkey with Mediterranean Rub

PREP 10 minutes **COOK** 3 to 3½ hours

MEDITERRANEAN RUB

- 1 **cup chopped fresh parsley**
- ¼ **cup ground dry lemon peel**
- 4 **teaspoons sugar**
- 4 **teaspoons sea salt**
- 4 **teaspoons chopped fresh rosemary**
- 1 **tablespoon dried oregano**
- 2 **teaspoons black pepper**
- ½ **teaspoon crushed red pepper flakes**

TURKEY

- 1 **(14- to 16-pound) BUTTERBALL® Fresh or Frozen Whole Turkey, thawed if frozen**

  Nonstick cooking spray

1. Preheat oven to 325°F. Combine parsley, lemon peel, sugar, salt, rosemary, oregano, black pepper and red pepper flakes in medium bowl; mix well. Cover; set aside.

2. Remove neck and giblets from body and neck cavities of turkey. Refrigerate for another use or discard. Pat turkey dry with paper towels. Turn wings back to hold neck skin in place. Return legs to the tucked position, if untucked. Place turkey, breast side up, on flat rack in shallow roasting pan. Coat evenly with cooking spray.

3. Roast turkey 1½ hours. Then, cover breast and top of drumsticks loosely with aluminum foil to prevent overcooking. Continue roasting turkey 1½ to 2 hours* or until meat thermometer reaches 180°F when inserted into deepest part of thigh not touching bone.

4. Transfer turkey to cutting board; loosely tent with foil. Let turkey stand 15 minutes before sprinkling rub over entire turkey and carving.**

Follow cooking times according to package directions; times vary with size of turkey.

**Or sprinkle on turkey slices after carving.*

Makes 12 to 14 servings

the whole *turkey*

Bourbon and Cola Marinated Roast Turkey

PREP 5 minutes   **MARINATE** 6 to 8 hours   **COOK** 3 to 3½ hours

BOURBON AND COLA MARINADE

- ¾ **cup cola soda***
- ½ **cup bourbon**
- ⅓ **cup fresh lemon juice**
- ⅓ **cup soy sauce**
- ¼ **cup chopped green onion**
- 1 **tablespoon minced garlic**
- ½ **teaspoon crushed red pepper flakes**

TURKEY

- 1 **(12- to 14-pound) BUTTERBALL® Fresh or Frozen Whole Turkey, thawed if frozen**

  Nonstick cooking spray

*Do not use diet or low-calorie soda.

1. Combine soda, bourbon, lemon juice, soy sauce, green onion, garlic and red pepper flakes in large nonmetallic container; mix well.

2. Remove neck and giblets from body and neck cavities of turkey. Refrigerate for another use or discard. Pat turkey dry with paper towels. Place turkey, breast side down, in marinade. Cover; refrigerate 6 to 8 hours, turning turkey over occasionally.

3. Preheat oven to 325°F. Remove turkey from marinade; discard marinade. Pat turkey dry with paper towels. Turn wings back to hold neck skin in place. Return legs to tucked position, if untucked. Place turkey, breast side up, on flat rack in shallow roasting pan; coat evenly with cooking spray.

4. Roast turkey 1½ hours. Then, cover breast and top of drumsticks loosely with aluminum foil to prevent overcooking.

5. Continue roasting turkey 1½ to 2 hours* or until meat thermometer reaches 180°F when inserted into deepest part of thigh not touching bone.

6. Transfer turkey to cutting board; loosely tent with foil. Let stand 15 minutes before carving.

*Follow cooking times according to package directions; times vary with size of turkey.

Makes 10 to 12 servings

the whole *turkey*

Roast Turkey with Spicy Rub

PREP 10 minutes   **CHILL** 12 hours   **COOK** 3 to 3½ hours

SPICY RUB

- 3 tablespoons firmly packed light brown sugar
- 3 tablespoons kosher or sea salt
- 3 tablespoons chili powder
- 2 teaspoons black pepper
- 2 teaspoons roasted ground cumin
- 2 teaspoons garlic powder
- 2 teaspoons crushed red pepper flakes
- 1 teaspoon ground coriander

TURKEY

- 1 (14- to 16-pound) BUTTERBALL® Fresh or Frozen Whole Turkey, thawed if frozen
- 6 tablespoons canola oil, divided

1. Combine brown sugar, salt, chili powder, black pepper, cumin, garlic powder, red pepper flakes and coriander in small bowl; mix well.

2. Remove neck and giblets from body and neck cavities of turkey. Refrigerate for another use or discard. Pat turkey dry with paper towels. Turn wings back to hold neck skin in place. Return legs to the tucked position, if untucked. Place turkey, breast side up, on flat rack in shallow roasting pan. Brush with 3 tablespoons oil. Apply prepared rub on skin and inside cavity. Cover; refrigerate at least 12 hours or overnight.

3. Preheat oven to 325°F. Brush outside of turkey with remaining 3 tablespoons oil.

4. Roast turkey 1½ hours. Then, cover breast and top of drumsticks loosely with aluminum foil to prevent overcooking. Continue roasting turkey 1½ to 2 hours* or until meat thermometer reaches 180°F when inserted into deepest part of thigh not touching bone.

5. Transfer turkey to cutting board; loosely tent with foil. Let stand 15 minutes before carving.

Follow cooking times according to package directions; times vary with size of turkey.

Makes 12 to 14 servings

the whole *turkey*

Maple Mustard Glazed Turkey

PREP 10 minutes   **COOK** 3 to 3½ hours

- ½ **cup maple syrup**
- ⅓ **cup Dijon mustard**
- ¼ **teaspoon garlic powder**
- ¼ **teaspoon black pepper**
- 1 **(12- to 14-pound) BUTTERBALL® Fresh or Frozen Whole Turkey, thawed if frozen**

1. Preheat oven to 325°F. Combine maple syrup, mustard, garlic powder and pepper in small bowl; mix well. Set aside.

2. Remove neck and giblets from body and neck cavities of turkey. Refrigerate for another use or discard. Pat turkey dry with paper towels. Turn wings back to hold neck skin in place. Return legs to the tucked position, if untucked. Place turkey, breast side up, on flat rack in shallow roasting pan.

3. Roast turkey 2 hours. Then, brush evenly with glaze. Cover breast and top of drumsticks loosely with aluminum foil to prevent overcooking. Continue roasting turkey 30 minutes. Uncover, brush with additional glaze, and return foil to cover breast and top of drumsticks.

4. Continue roasting turkey about 1 hour* or until meat thermometer reaches 180°F when inserted into deepest part of thigh not touching bone.

5. Transfer turkey to cutting board; loosely tent with foil. Let stand 15 minutes before carving.

Follow cooking times according to package directions; times vary with size of turkey.

Makes 12 servings

*everyday **entrées***

Turkey Pomodoro

PREP 30 minutes   **COOK** 10 minutes

SAUCE

- ⅓ cup olive oil
- 3 tablespoons minced garlic
- 8 cups diced plum tomatoes with juice
- 1 cup chopped fresh Italian parsley
- 1 cup pitted chopped kalamata olives
- ⅓ cup chopped fresh basil leaves
- 3 bay leaves
- 2 teaspoons dried oregano
- 2 teaspoons sugar

PASTA

- 1¼ pounds leftover cooked BUTTERBALL® Turkey, cut into ¼-inch strips
- 1¼ pounds (6 cups) rigatoni pasta, cooked and drained
- 6 tablespoons grated Parmesan cheese
- 6 tablespoons chopped fresh Italian parsley

1. Heat oil in large saucepan over medium heat. Add garlic; cook and stir 30 seconds. Add tomatoes, 1 cup parsley, olives, basil, bay leaves, oregano and sugar; stir well. Bring to a boil. Reduce heat and simmer, uncovered, 5 minutes.

2. Add turkey to pasta sauce. Return to a boil and heat through. Remove bay leaves before serving.

3. Place pasta in large serving bowl. Top with pasta sauce, cheese and 6 tablespoons parsley.

Makes 6 servings

Chili Wagon Wheel Casserole

PREP 5 minutes   **COOK** 15 minutes   **BAKE** 25 minutes

8 ounces wagon wheel or other pasta, cooked and drained

1 package (16 ounces) BUTTERBALL® Fresh Ground Turkey

¾ cup chopped onion

¾ cup chopped green bell pepper

1 can (about 14 ounces) no-salt-added stewed tomatoes

1 can (8 ounces) no-salt-added tomato sauce

½ teaspoon black pepper

¼ teaspoon ground allspice

½ cup (2 ounces) shredded Cheddar cheese

1. Preheat oven to 350°F.

2. Lightly coat large nonstick skillet with nonstick cooking spray; heat over medium-high heat. Add turkey; cook and stir 5 to 6 minutes until no longer pink (165°F). Add onion and bell pepper; cook and stir until tender.

3. Stir in tomatoes, tomato sauce, black pepper and allspice; cook 2 minutes. Stir in pasta. Spoon mixture into 2½-quart casserole. Sprinkle with cheese.

4. Bake 20 to 25 minutes or until heated through.

Makes 6 servings

everyday entrées

Spicy Turkey with Citrus au Jus

PREP 10 minutes   **COOK** 4 to 5 hours (LOW) or 2½ to 3 hours (HIGH)

1 **(4-pound) BUTTERBALL® Fresh or Frozen Whole Turkey Breast, thawed, if frozen, rinsed and patted dry**

¼ **cup (½ stick) butter, softened**

Zest of 1 lemon

1 **teaspoon chili powder**

¼ **to ½ teaspoon black pepper**

⅛ **to ¼ teaspoon red pepper flakes**

1 **tablespoon lemon juice**

SLOW COOKER DIRECTIONS

1. Lightly coat slow cooker with nonstick cooking spray. Remove and discard turkey skin. Place turkey breast in slow cooker.

2. Combine butter, lemon peel, chili powder, black pepper and red pepper flakes in small bowl; mix well. Spread over top and sides of turkey. Cover; cook on LOW 4 to 5 hours or on HIGH 2½ to 3 hours or until temperature registers 170°F on meat thermometer inserted into thickest part of breast not touching bone.

3. Transfer turkey to cutting board; let stand 10 minutes before slicing.

4. Stir lemon juice into cooking liquid. Strain; discard solids. Let mixture stand 15 minutes. Skim and discard excess fat. Serve with turkey.

Makes 6 to 8 servings

*everyday **entrées***

Turkey and Mushroom Stroganoff

PREP 15 minutes   **COOK** 25 minutes

- 5 **tablespoons butter, divided**
- 2 **teaspoons minced garlic**
- 2 **cups diced onions**
- 3 **cups sliced mushrooms**
- ½ **teaspoon black pepper**
- ¾ **cup dry white wine**
- 3 **cups prepared brown sauce***
- 2 **pounds shredded leftover cooked BUTTERBALL® Turkey**
- 2 **cups sour cream**
- ⅓ **cup chopped fresh dill**
- 8 **ounces (4 cups) uncooked egg noodles**

*Use purchased gravy from supermarket or gourmet shop, or prepare from dry mix.

1. Melt 3 tablespoons butter in large saucepan over medium heat. Add garlic; cook and stir 30 seconds. Add onions; cook and stir 8 minutes. Add mushrooms and pepper; cook and stir 3 to 5 minutes or until mushrooms are light golden brown. Add white wine; bring to a boil. Reduce heat to medium-low; simmer, uncovered, 10 minutes or until reduced by half.

2. Stir in brown sauce; bring to a boil. Reduce heat and simmer, uncovered, 3 minutes. Stir in turkey; heat through. Remove from heat; stir in sour cream and dill.

3. Meanwhile, cook noodles according to package directions; drain. Toss with remaining 2 tablespoons butter. Place on serving plate. Top with stroganoff mixture.

Makes 6 servings

*everyday **entrées***

Classic Smoked Sausage Mac and Cheese

PREP 5 minutes   **COOK** 15 minutes   **BAKE** 25 minutes

1 **pound cavatappi (corkscrew) pasta, cooked and drained**

¼ **cup (½ stick) plus 1 tablespoon butter, melted, divided**

1 **package (14 ounces) BUTTERBALL® Smoked Turkey Dinner Sausage, cut in half lengthwise, then cut diagonally into ¼-inch slices**

1 **cup chopped onions**

3 **cups prepared Alfredo sauce**

3 **cups half-and-half**

1½ **pounds pasteurized prepared cheese product, cut into cubes**

2 **cups (8 ounces) shredded sharp Cheddar cheese**

½ **teaspoon black pepper**

1 **cup panko bread crumbs**

1. Preheat oven to 375°F. Coat 13×9-inch baking dish with nonstick cooking spray.

2. Heat 1 tablespoon butter in large saucepan over medium heat. Add sausage and onions; cook and stir 3 to 5 minutes or until onions are tender. Stir in Alfredo sauce and half-and-half. Bring to a boil, stirring constantly. Reduce heat; simmer 1 minute.

3. Remove from heat. Add cheese cubes, shredded Cheddar cheese and pepper; stir until cheese is melted. Add pasta; mix well. Pour into prepared baking dish. Combine bread crumbs and remaining ¼ cup melted butter in small bowl. Sprinkle evenly over top of mixture.

4. Bake 20 to 25 minutes or until hot and bubbly and crumbs are golden brown.

Makes 10 servings

Serving suggestion: Serve with a green salad to round out the meal.

*everyday **entrées***

Turkey, Cheddar and Vegetable Frittata

PREP 10 minutes   **COOK** 2 minutes   **BAKE** 8 minutes

12 large eggs

1½ cups diced leftover cooked BUTTERBALL® Turkey

1 cup diced leftover cooked vegetables

1 cup (4 ounces) shredded Cheddar cheese

3 tablespoons olive oil

¼ cup shredded or grated Parmesan cheese

1. Preheat oven to 350°F. Beat eggs in large bowl. Stir in turkey, vegetables and Cheddar cheese.

2. Heat oil in 12-inch ovenproof skillet over medium-high heat. Pour in egg mixture. Cook 2 to 3 minutes or until eggs start to set around edges of skillet.

3. Place in oven. Bake 8 to 10 minutes or until top is firm and sides begin to pull away from edges.

4. Remove skillet from oven. Invert frittata onto serving platter. Before serving, sprinkle with Parmesan cheese.

Makes 8 servings

Turkey and Jasmine Rice Stuffed Peppers

PREP 30 minutes   **BAKE** 1½ hours

  2 **tablespoons olive oil**
  1 **tablespoon minced garlic**
  2 **cups diced onions**
  ½ **cup diced carrots**
1½ **pounds diced leftover cooked BUTTERBALL® Turkey**
2¾ **cups chicken broth, divided**
  2 **cups cooked jasmine rice**
  1 **cup grated Parmesan cheese**
  1 **cup chopped fresh Italian parsley**

  ¾ **cup dry unseasoned bread crumbs**
  3 **eggs, beaten**
  1 **tablespoon chopped fresh sage**
  1 **tablespoon chopped fresh thyme**
  4 **red or green bell peppers, cut in half and seeds removed**
  4 **cups Italian tomato sauce**
  2 **bay leaves**

1. Preheat oven to 325°F. Heat oil in medium skillet over medium heat. Add garlic; cook and stir 30 seconds. Add onions and carrots; cook and stir 3 minutes. Spoon mixture into large bowl.

2. Add turkey, ¾ cup broth, rice, cheese, parsley, bread crumbs, eggs, sage and thyme; mix well. Divide evenly among bell pepper halves. Place filled bell peppers in large baking pan.

3. Blend tomato sauce and remaining 2 cups broth. Stir in bay leaves. Spoon sauce evenly over and around bell peppers.

4. Bake 1¼ to 1½ hours or until bell peppers are tender. Remove bay leaves before serving.

Makes 4 servings

*everyday **entrées***

Smoked Sausage with Mediterranean-Style Vegetables

PREP 10 minutes   **MARINATE** 30 minutes   **COOK** 10 to 20 minutes

2 zucchini, sliced lengthwise into ½-inch slices, then cut in half

6 slices eggplant, ¾ inch thick

2 red onions, sliced ½ inch thick

2 tomatoes, sliced ½ inch thick

½ cup reduced-fat balsamic vinaigrette dressing

1 package (14 ounces) BUTTERBALL® Polska Kielbasa Turkey Dinner Sausage

3 ounces crumbled feta cheese

6 fresh basil leaves

½ cup reduced-fat red wine vinaigrette

1. Place zucchini, eggplant, onions and tomatoes in resealable plastic food storage bag or glass dish. Add balsamic vinaigrette; seal bag and toss to coat vegetables evenly. Refrigerate 30 minutes to marinate.

2. Preheat grill to medium.

3. Remove vegetables from marinade. Grill sausage, zucchini, eggplant and onions 8 to 10 minutes, turning frequently until sausage is heated through and vegetables are tender. Add tomatoes during last 2 minutes of cooking, turning after 1 minute.

4. Cut sausage into diagonal slices. Divide sausage and vegetables evenly among serving plates. Top with cheese and basil leaves. Drizzle with red wine vinaigrette.

Makes 6 servings

*everyday **entrées***

Italian Turkey Sausage Stew

PREP 10 minutes   **COOK** 20 minutes

3 links BUTTERBALL® Fresh Hot
   Italian Turkey Sausage (about
   9 ounces), casings removed

1 green bell pepper, chopped

2 cloves garlic, minced

1 can (about 15 ounces)
   no-salt-added navy beans,
   rinsed and drained

1 can (about 14 ounces)
   Italian-style stewed tomatoes

1 cup turkey or chicken broth

1 teaspoon dried rosemary

1. Cook and stir turkey sausage in large saucepan over medium-high heat 6 to 8 minutes or until no longer pink (165°F). Drain any fat.

2. Add bell pepper and garlic; cook and stir 1 minute or until garlic is fragrant. Add beans, tomatoes, broth and rosemary; bring to a simmer. Cover; simmer over medium-low heat 5 minutes or until bell pepper is tender.

Makes 4 servings

*everyday **entrées***

Pastitsio

PREP 5 minutes   **COOK** 20 minutes   **BAKE** 40 minutes

8 ounces elbow macaroni, cooked
  and drained

2 eggs, lightly beaten, or ½ cup
  cholesterol-free egg substitute

¼ teaspoon ground nutmeg

1 package (16 ounces)
  BUTTERBALL® Fresh
  Ground Turkey

½ cup chopped onion

1 clove garlic, minced

1 can (8 ounces) tomato sauce

¾ teaspoon dried mint

½ teaspoon dried oregano

½ teaspoon black pepper

⅛ teaspoon ground cinnamon

2 teaspoons butter or margarine

3 tablespoons all-purpose flour

1½ cups fat-free (skim) milk

2 tablespoons grated Parmesan
  cheese

1. Preheat oven to 350°F. Lightly coat 9-inch square baking dish with nonstick cooking spray.

2. Combine macaroni, eggs and nutmeg in prepared baking dish; mix well.

3. Cook and stir turkey, onion and garlic in large nonstick skillet over medium heat 6 to 8 minutes or until turkey is no longer pink (165°F). Stir in tomato sauce, mint, oregano, pepper and cinnamon. Reduce heat; simmer 10 minutes. Spread evenly over macaroni in baking dish.

4. Melt butter in small saucepan. Add flour; cook and stir 1 minute. Whisk in milk; cook 6 minutes or until thickened, stirring constantly. Pour sauce over meat mixture. Sprinkle with cheese.

5. Bake 30 to 40 minutes. Let stand 10 minutes before serving.

Makes 6 servings

Tex-Mex Turkey Rice Skillet

PREP 10 minutes   **COOK** 20 minutes

2 **tablespoons vegetable oil, divided**

1 **cup uncooked long-grain rice**

1 **can (about 14 ounces) chicken broth**

1 **cup medium or hot chunky salsa**

2 **cups chopped zucchini**

½ **cup chopped onion**

1 **cup frozen corn**

1½ **cups chopped leftover cooked BUTTERBALL® Turkey**

1 **cup (4 ounces) shredded Mexican-style cheese**

1. Heat 1 tablespoon oil in large skillet over medium heat. Add rice; cook and stir about 3 minutes or until rice turns light golden brown. Stir in broth and salsa. Cover; reduce heat to low and simmer 15 minutes or until rice is tender.

2. Meanwhile, heat remaining 1 tablespoon oil in another skillet over medium-high heat. Add zucchini and onion; cook and stir 3 minutes. Add corn; cook and stir 2 minutes or until vegetables just start to brown on edges. Stir in turkey; cover and keep warm until rice is done.

3. Add turkey mixture to cooked rice; cook 2 minutes or until heated through, stirring occasionally. Sprinkle evenly with cheese; cover. Remove from heat; let stand 5 minutes or until cheese is melted.

Makes 4 servings

*everyday **entrées***

Turkey Burgers with Creole Gravy

PREP 15 minutes   **COOK** 10 to 20 minutes

CREOLE GRAVY

- 3 **tablespoons butter**
- 1 **tablespoon minced garlic**
- 1 **cup diced green bell peppers**
- 1 **cup diced onions**
- ½ **cup diced celery**
- 1 **can (about 14 ounces) fire-roasted diced tomatoes, undrained**
- 1 **jar (about 12 ounces) prepared turkey gravy**
- 3 **tablespoons Cajun seasoning**
- 1 **tablespoon Worcestershire sauce**

TURKEY BURGERS

- 1 **package (16 ounces) BUTTERBALL® Fresh All Natural Turkey Burger Patties**
- 4 **slices warm French bread, cut diagonally**

1. Melt butter in 2-quart saucepan over medium-high heat. Add garlic; cook and stir 1 minute. Add bell peppers, onions and celery; cook and stir 5 minutes. Add tomatoes, gravy, Cajun seasoning and Worcestershire sauce. Bring to a boil. Reduce heat; simmer, uncovered, 15 minutes.

2. Coat medium skillet with nonstick cooking spray; heat over medium heat. Place patties in skillet; cook 4 to 5 minutes on each side, or until meat thermometer inserted in centers reaches 165°F.

3. Place 1 bread slice on each serving plate. Top with burger; serve with gravy.

Makes 4 servings

lighter anytime meals

Turkey French Dip Panini

PREP 15 minutes   **COOK** 6 minutes

1 **(6-inch) French bread roll, cut in half horizontally**	¼ **cup sliced sautéed onions**
2 **teaspoons olive oil**	4 **ounces thinly sliced leftover cooked BUTTERBALL® Turkey**
1 **tablespoon Dijon-style mayonnaise**	2 **slices Asiago cheese**
1 **tablespoon olive-oil mayonnaise**	⅓ **cup turkey gravy, heated**

1. Brush outside top and bottom crusts of roll with olive oil.

2. Spread cut side of roll bottom with Dijon-style mayonnaise; spread cut side of roll top with olive-oil mayonnaise.

3. Place onions on roll bottom; top with turkey and cheese. Cover with roll top.

4. Grill in heated panini grill 4 to 6 minutes or until golden brown on both sides and cheese is melted. Cut sandwich in half; serve with gravy for dipping.

Makes 1 serving

tip

If you don't have a panini grill, coat a large heavy skillet or stovetop grill pan with nonstick cooking spray; heat over medium-low heat. Add the assembled panini. Weigh it down with a heatproof platter (if necessary, add a can or other weight to press down). Cook over low heat 3 to 4 minutes. Remove platter using oven mitt and turn over panini. Press down again; cook 3 minutes or just until cheese melts.

lighter anytime meals

Wild Rice and Turkey Soup

PREP 20 minutes   **COOK** 20 minutes

- 1 **tablespoon vegetable oil**
- 1 **cup finely chopped carrots**
- 1 **cup finely chopped onions**
- ½ **cup finely chopped celery**
- 2 **cloves garlic, minced**
- 2 **cans (about 14 ounces each) chicken broth**
- 2 **cups chopped leftover cooked BUTTERBALL® Turkey**
- 2 **cups cooked wild rice**
- ¼ **teaspoon salt**
- ¼ **teaspoon black pepper**
- 2 **cups whipping cream**
- 2 **tablespoons dry sherry**

1. Heat oil in large saucepan over medium-high heat. Add carrots, onions, celery and garlic. Cook and stir 5 minutes or until vegetables are tender.

2. Stir in broth, turkey, rice, salt and pepper. Cook 10 minutes, stirring occasionally.

3. Stir in cream and sherry. Cook until heated through, stirring occasionally. Serve immediately.

Makes 8 servings

lighter anytime meals

Savory Turkey Chili

PREP 20 minutes **COOK** 30 minutes

2 tablespoons canola oil
2 teaspoons minced garlic
1 cup diced onions
2 tablespoons seeded diced
   jalapeño pepper*
2 teaspoons chili powder
2 teaspoons roasted ground cumin
2½ cups chopped leftover cooked
   BUTTERBALL® Turkey
2 cans (15 ounces each) red kidney
   beans, rinsed and drained

2 cups chicken broth
1 can (4 ounces) chopped mild
   green chiles, drained
¼ cup chopped fresh cilantro
6 tablespoons sour cream
6 tablespoons shredded Cheddar
   cheese or Monterey Jack cheese
6 tablespoons sliced green onions
   Oyster crackers (optional)

Jalapeño peppers can sting and irritate the skin, so wear rubber gloves when handling peppers and do not touch your eyes.

1. Heat oil in large saucepan over medium heat. Add garlic; cook and stir 30 seconds. Add onions; cook and stir 3 minutes.

2. Remove from heat. Stir in jalapeño pepper, chili powder and cumin. Return to heat. Stir in turkey, beans, broth, chiles and cilantro; bring to a boil. Reduce heat and simmer, uncovered, 25 minutes.

3. To serve, divide chili evenly among six bowls. Top each serving with 1 tablespoon sour cream, 1 tablespoon cheese and 1 tablespoon green onion. Serve with crackers, if desired.

Makes 6 servings

Soft Turkey Tacos

PREP 5 minutes   **COOK** 15 minutes

 8 **(6-inch) corn tortillas***
1½ **teaspoons vegetable oil**
 1 **package (16 ounces) BUTTERBALL® Fresh Ground Turkey**
 1 **small onion, chopped**
 1 **teaspoon dried oregano**
    Salt, to taste
    Black pepper, to taste
    Chopped tomatoes
    Shredded lettuce
    Salsa
    Refried beans (optional)

*Substitute 8 (10-inch) flour tortillas for corn tortillas, if desired.

1. Wrap tortillas in aluminum foil. Place in cold oven; heat to 350°F.

2. Heat oil in large skillet over medium heat. Add turkey and onion; cook and stir until turkey is no longer pink (165°F). Stir in oregano. Season with salt and pepper.

3. Remove tortillas from oven and fill with turkey mixture; top with tomatoes, lettuce and salsa. Serve with refried beans, if desired.

Makes 4 servings

tip

To warm tortillas in microwave oven, wrap loosely in damp paper towel.

Microwave on HIGH 2 minutes or until hot.

lighter anytime meals

Barley Turkey Vegetable Salad

PREP 25 minutes   **COOK** 10 minutes

- 2 **cups water**
- ½ **teaspoon lemon pepper**
- 1 **cup uncooked quick pearl barley**
- 2 **cups chopped leftover cooked BUTTERBALL® Turkey**
- ½ **pound cooked fresh asparagus spears, cut into 1-inch pieces**
- 1 **cup shredded red cabbage**
- 1 **medium carrot, coarsely shredded**
- ¼ **cup sliced green onions**
- 2 **tablespoons olive oil**
- 2 **tablespoons lemon juice**
- 1 **tablespoon Dijon-style mustard**
- 1 **teaspoon sugar**
- ¼ **teaspoon salt**

1. Combine water and lemon pepper in medium saucepan; bring to a boil over medium-high heat. Stir in barley. Cover; reduce heat and simmer 10 minutes or until barley is tender. Remove from heat. Let stand, covered, 5 minutes. Drain if necessary. Place barley in large bowl; cool 10 minutes.

2. Add turkey, asparagus, cabbage, carrot and green onions; mix lightly.

3. Whisk oil, lemon juice, mustard, sugar and salt in small bowl until well blended. Pour dressing over barley mixture; mix lightly. Serve at room temperature.

Makes 6 servings

Franks Hawaiian-Style

PREP 10 minutes   **COOK** 10 minutes

6 **slices fresh or canned pineapple, drained**

2 **teaspoons vegetable oil**

1 **cup mango salsa**

1 **tablespoon chopped fresh cilantro**

2 **teaspoons pickled ginger**

1 **package (16 ounces) BUTTERBALL® Bun Size Premium Turkey Franks**

8 **hot dog buns, split and toasted**

3 **tablespoons Dijon-style mustard**

6 **slices BUTTERBALL® Turkey Bacon, cooked and crumbled**

1. Prepare grill for direct cooking over medium heat. Lightly brush pineapple with oil. Grill 1 to 2 minutes per side or until golden brown. Cut into ¼-inch pieces; place in medium bowl. Stir in salsa, cilantro and ginger. Refrigerate until ready to use.

2. Grill franks, turning frequently, 6 to 10 minutes or until heated through. Serve in buns with mustard and pineapple mixture; sprinkle evenly with turkey bacon.

Makes 8 servings

Turkey Club Salad

PREP 10 minutes

8 large romaine lettuce leaves
¼ pound sliced BUTTERBALL®
   Oven Roasted Turkey Breast
2 medium tomatoes, cut into
   8 slices each

2 tablespoons BUTTERBALL®
   Turkey Bacon, cooked, drained
   and diced
¼ cup fat-free ranch salad dressing
   Black pepper (optional)

Layer lettuce, turkey slices, tomato slices and turkey bacon on two plates. Drizzle with dressing or serve dressing on the side. Season with pepper, if desired.

Makes 2 servings

lighter anytime meals

Veggie-Packed Turkey Burgers

PREP 10 minutes   **COOK** 10 minutes

- **1 package (16 ounces) BUTTERBALL® Fresh Ground Turkey**
- **½ cup chopped onion**
- **½ cup shredded zucchini**
- **½ cup shredded carrots**
- **1 teaspoon minced jalapeño pepper***
- **Salt, to taste**
- **Black pepper, to taste**
- **Whole wheat rolls or hamburger buns**
- **Shredded lettuce**
- **Tomato slices**

*Jalapeño peppers can sting and irritate the skin, so wear rubber gloves when handling peppers and do not touch your eyes.

1. Coat grill grid with nonstick cooking spray. Prepare grill for direct cooking.

2. Combine turkey, onion, zucchini, carrots, jalapeño pepper, salt and black pepper in large bowl. Form 4 (½-inch-thick) patties.

3. Grill, covered, 4 to 5 minutes per side over medium-high heat or until no longer pink and center of burgers reaches 165°F as measured with meat thermometer. Serve on topped with lettuce and tomato slices.

Makes 4 servings

Thai Turkey Wrap

PREP 15 minutes

3 tablespoons mayonnaise	¾ cup leftover cooked BUTTERBALL® Turkey, cut into 1×¼-inch strips
¾ teaspoon prepared garlic chili sauce	
1 (10-inch) flour tortilla	2 tablespoons prepared spicy peanut sauce
⅓ cup shredded lettuce	
3 tablespoons shredded carrot	Additional prepared spicy peanut sauce (optional)
2 tablespoons thinly sliced green onion	

1. Combine mayonnaise and chili sauce in small bowl. Heat tortilla in skillet or microwave about 10 seconds.

2. Spread one side of tortilla with mayonnaise mixture. Place lettuce down center; top with carrot, green onion, turkey and 2 tablespoons peanut sauce.

3. Fold bottom half of tortilla over filling; fold sides toward center, leaving top open. Serve with additional peanut sauce, if desired.

Makes 1 serving

tip

To make this wrap for a lunch box, fold it to enclose the filling completely: fold in two sides, then roll the tortilla up tightly from the bottom.

lighter anytime meals

Toasted Cobb Salad Sandwiches

PREP 5 minutes   **COOK** 10 minutes

½ **medium avocado**
1 **green onion, chopped**
½ **teaspoon lemon juice**
   Salt, to taste
   Black pepper, to taste
2 **Kaiser rolls, split**
¼ **pound thinly sliced BUTTERBALL® Oven Roasted Turkey Breast**
4 **slices BUTTERBALL® Fully Cooked Turkey Bacon**
1 **hard-cooked egg, sliced**
2 **slices (1 ounce each) Cheddar cheese**
2 **ounces blue cheese**
   Tomato slices (optional)
   Olive oil

1. Mash avocado in small bowl; stir in green onion and lemon juice. Season with salt and pepper. Spread avocado mixture on cut side of top half of each Kaiser roll.

2. Layer turkey slices, turkey bacon, egg, Cheddar cheese, blue cheese and tomato, if desired, on bottom half of each roll. Cover each with top of roll. Brush outsides of sandwiches lightly with oil.

3. Heat large nonstick skillet over medium heat. Add sandwiches; cook 4 to 5 minutes per side or until cheese melts and sandwiches are golden brown.

Makes 2 sandwiches

lighter anytime meals

Carolina Turkey Burger

PREP 10 minutes   **COOK** 20 minutes

---

4 **BUTTERBALL® Original Seasoned Frozen Turkey Burgers**

½ **cup prepared barbecue sauce**

8 **slices (½ ounce each) Cheddar cheese**

¼ **cup Dijon-style mayonnaise**

4 **hamburger buns, split, buttered and toasted**

1⅓ **cups prepared coleslaw**

1. Prepare turkey burgers according to package directions for broiling.

2. When burgers are heated, top each with 1 tablespoon barbecue sauce and 2 slices cheese. Broil 1 minute or until cheese is melted.

3. Spread 1 tablespoon mayonnaise on bottom half of each hamburger bun. Top each with 1 cheese-topped burger and ⅓ cup coleslaw. Cover each with top of bun.

Makes 4 servings

Serving Suggestion:
For an easy change of pace, try cooking burgers on the grill according to package directions.

Mediterranean Turkey Pasta Salad

PREP 30 minutes

1½ **cups olive oil**

½ **cup red wine vinegar**

1 **tablespoon minced garlic**

2 **teaspoons dried oregano**

3 **cups diced leftover cooked BUTTERBALL® Turkey**

3 **cups cooked penne pasta**

1 **jar (16 ounces) pitted kalamata olives, drained and chopped**

1 **container (10 ounces) grape tomatoes, cut in half**

8 **ounces crumbled feta cheese**

1 **package (6 ounces) spring salad mix**

½ **cup chopped fresh Italian parsley**

½ **cup thinly sliced red onion**

1. Whisk oil, vinegar, garlic and oregano in small bowl until well blended.

2. Combine turkey, pasta, olives, tomatoes, cheese, salad greens, parsley and red onion in large salad bowl. Gently toss with dressing. Refrigerate or serve at room temperature.

Makes 6 servings

savory *side dishes*

Sautéed Green Beans with Crunchy Almonds

PREP 15 minutes   **CHILL** 1 hour   **COOK** 10 minutes

- 2 **pounds green beans, trimmed**
- 3 **tablespoons unsalted butter**
- 1 **tablespoon olive oil**
- ½ **cup toasted slivered almonds***
- 2 **tablespoons chopped fresh parsley**

*To toast almonds, spread in single layer in heavy-bottomed skillet. Cook over medium heat 1 to 2 minutes, stirring frequently, until nuts are lightly browned. Remove from skillet immediately. Cool before using.

1. Place green beans in large saucepan with enough water to cover. Bring to a boil over medium-high heat. Reduce heat to medium-low; simmer, uncovered, 4 to 6 minutes or until beans reach desired tenderness.

2. Drain beans and immerse in ice water. Let stand 3 to 5 minutes or until completely chilled. Drain; pat dry with paper towels. Place in resealable plastic food storage bag. Refrigerate at least 1 hour.

3. Heat butter and oil in large skillet over medium heat until butter is melted. Add beans; cook and stir 4 to 6 minutes or until light golden brown. Stir in almonds and parsley. Heat through and serve warm.

Makes 8 servings

tip

Green beans can be boiled up one day in advance. Cool and refrigerate as directed in step 2, then proceed as directed when ready to serve.

Whipped Potatoes with Roasted Cauliflower

PREP 20 minutes   **COOK** 45 minutes

- **1 large head cauliflower, cleaned and cut into florets**
- **7 tablespoons olive oil, divided**
- **3¾ teaspoons sea salt, divided**
- **1 tablespoon minced garlic**
- **¾ teaspoon black pepper**
- **3½ pounds Yukon Gold potatoes, peeled and cut into quarters**
- **1½ cups warm milk**
- **¼ cup (½ stick) butter, softened**

1. Preheat oven to 400°F.

2. Place cauliflower in large bowl. Toss with 3 tablespoons oil, ¾ teaspoon salt, garlic and pepper. Transfer to 13×9-inch pan. Bake 40 to 45 minutes or until cauliflower is golden brown, stirring halfway through baking time. Remove from oven; cover with aluminum foil to keep warm.

3. Meanwhile, place potatoes in large saucepan with enough water to cover; stir in remaining 3 teaspoons salt. Bring to a boil over medium-high heat. Reduce heat to medium-low; simmer, uncovered, 15 to 20 minutes or until potatoes are tender when pierced with fork.

4. Drain potatoes; place in large bowl. Add remaining 4 tablespoons oil, milk and butter. Mash to smooth consistency. Fold in roasted cauliflower.

Makes 12 servings

Lemony Pan-Grilled Asparagus with Olive Oil

PREP 10 minutes   **COOK** 5 to 7 minutes

3 **pounds fresh asparagus, trimmed**
¼ **cup olive oil**
3 **tablespoons lemon zest**
   Lemon peel strips (optional)

1. Heat lightly oiled stovetop grilling pan over medium-high heat 3 to 4 minutes or until hot.

2. Dry asparagus with paper towels. Working in batches, place on hot pan.

Turn asparagus to ensure grill marks on all sides. Cook and turn until crisp-tender. (Time will vary depending on thickness of asparagus.) Keep cooked asparagus warm. Repeat with remaining asparagus.

3. Arrange on serving platter. Drizzle with oil and sprinkle with lemon zest. Garnish with lemon peel strips.

Makes 10 servings

savory *side dishes*

Turkey Pan Gravy

PREP 10 minutes   **COOK** 20 minutes

¼ **cup defatted turkey pan drippings**
½ **cup all-purpose flour**
½ **teaspoon poultry seasoning**
¼ **teaspoon salt**
¼ **teaspoon black pepper**
3¾ **cups chicken broth**

1. Place pan drippings in medium saucepan. Add flour, seasoning, salt and pepper; mix until smooth. Gradually whisk in broth until smooth.

2. Bring to a boil over medium heat, stirring occasionally. Reduce heat to medium-low; simmer 5 minutes, stirring frequently, until gravy is thickened.

Makes 12 servings

tip

For a different flavor, substitute dry white wine for part of the broth, if desired. You can also increase the amount of poultry seasoning, to taste.

savory *side dishes*

Bread Stuffing

PREP 20 minutes **BAKE** 1 hour

1½ pounds French bread, cut into 1-inch cubes	2 tablespoons fresh thyme
¾ cup (1½ sticks) butter	10 fresh sage leaves, chopped
1 clove garlic, minced	1 teaspoon salt
1½ cups diced celery	1 teaspoon black pepper
1½ cups diced onions	4 cups chicken broth
3 fresh bay leaves, chopped	3 large eggs, beaten
	⅓ cup chopped fresh Italian parsley

1. Preheat oven to 350°F. Butter 3-quart covered casserole dish. Place bread cubes in single layer on large baking sheet. Bake 8 to 10 minutes or until bread is golden brown, stirring once during baking. Cool on wire rack.

2. Melt butter in large skillet over medium heat. Add garlic; cook and stir 1 minute. Add celery, onions and bay leaves; cook and stir 6 to 8 minutes or until vegetables are soft. Add thyme, sage, salt and pepper; cook and stir 1 minute.

3. Combine broth and eggs in medium bowl. Place toasted bread in large bowl; stir in parsley and cooked vegetable mixture. Add three-fourths of broth mixture; stir in gently. Stuffing should be moist but not wet; add remaining broth mixture as necessary. Spoon stuffing into prepared casserole dish.

4. Cover; bake 30 minutes. Remove cover; bake 20 to 30 minutes longer or until top of stuffing is golden brown and crisp; center of stuffing should reach 165°F.

Makes 12 servings

savory *side dishes*

Fresh Cranberry Sauce with Port Wine

PREP 10 minutes   **COOK** 20 minutes   **CHILL** 2 to 3 hours

SPICE BUNDLE

- 1 piece cheesecloth, 10 inches square
- 18 whole allspice berries
- 1 3-inch cinnamon stick, broken in half
- 8 whole black peppercorns
- 6 whole cloves
- 4 to 5 inches food-safe string

CRANBERRY SAUCE

- 1 package (12 ounces) fresh whole cranberries
- 1 Honey Crisp apple, peeled and diced
- 1 cup firmly packed light brown sugar

- 1 cup fresh orange juice
- 2 tablespoons fresh lemon juice
- ⅓ cup port wine

1. Spread cheesecloth on work surface. Place allspice, cinnamon, peppercorns and cloves in center; bring up sides to form bundle. Tie tightly with string.

2. Combine cranberries, apple, brown sugar, orange juice, lemon juice and prepared spice bundle in large saucepan; stir well. Bring to a boil over medium-high heat. Reduce heat to medium-low; simmer, uncovered, 15 to 20 minutes or until cranberries begin to pop and mixture thickens slightly, stirring frequently.

3. Remove and discard spice bundle. Refrigerate cranberry sauce in covered container 2 to 3 hours or until well chilled.*

4. Before serving, gently stir wine into cranberry sauce.

Cranberry sauce can be prepared the day before and refrigerated overnight.

Makes 12 servings

Baked Acorn Squash with Brown Sugar and Butter

PREP 15 minutes   **BAKE** 1 hour 5 minutes

⅓ **cup firmly packed brown sugar**

4 **teaspoons ground cinnamon**

4 **acorn squash (each about 1½ pounds), cut in half lengthwise, seeds removed**

½ **cup (1 stick) butter**

1. Preheat oven to 375°F. Combine brown sugar and cinnamon in small bowl; set aside.

2. Trim thin slice off side or bottom of each squash half so squash will stay upright when served. Place squash halves, cavity side down, on two rimmed baking pans.

3. Bake 50 to 60 minutes or until knife can easily be inserted. Remove from oven. Turn over; pierce bottoms with fork. Sprinkle cavities evenly with cinnamon mixture. Place 1 tablespoon butter in each squash. Return to oven 3 to 5 minutes or until butter is melted. Serve warm.

Makes 8 servings

Asiago Whipped Potatoes with Turkey Bacon

PREP 10 minutes   **COOK** 15 minutes

2 **pounds red potatoes, peeled and cut in half**

1 **tablespoon olive oil**

1 **large leek, white part only, cut in half lengthwise and thinly sliced**

5 **ounces grated Asiago cheese**

2 **tablespoons butter, softened**

Salt, to taste

Black pepper, to taste

¾ **cup BUTTERBALL® Turkey Bacon, cut into ¼-inch pieces and cooked until crisp**

1. Place potatoes in large saucepan with enough water to cover. Bring to a boil over medium-high heat. Reduce heat to medium-low; simmer, uncovered, 10 to 15 minutes or until tender when pierced with fork.

2. Heat oil in small skillet over medium heat. Add leek; cook and stir 2 to 3 minutes or until tender but not brown. Set aside.

3. Drain potatoes, reserving cooking liquid. Add cheese, butter and leek to potatoes. Mash until fairly smooth, adding ½ to ¾ cup reserved cooking liquid if necessary for desired consistency. Season with salt and pepper. Fold in turkey bacon.

Makes 8 servings

Pound Cake with Limoncello and Sweet Spiced Apples

PREP 10 minutes   **COOK** 5 minutes

	Sweet Spiced Apples (recipe follows)
12	slices pound cake, cut ⅜ inch thick
¾	cup Limoncello
¾	cup whipped cream
¾	cup toasted chopped pecans*

*To toast pecans, spread in single layer in heavy-bottomed skillet. Cook over medium heat 1 to 2 minutes, stirring frequently, until nuts are lightly browned. Remove from skillet immediately. Cool before using.

1. Prepare Sweet Spiced Apples. Keep warm.

2. To serve, toast pound cake slices; place on dessert plates. Top each with large spoonful of Sweet Spiced Apples, 1 tablespoon Limoncello, 1 tablespoon whipped cream and 1 tablespoon nuts.

Makes 12 servings

Sweet Spiced Apples

⅓	cup unsalted butter
⅓	cup firmly packed brown sugar
2	teaspoons ground cinnamon
¼	teaspoon ground nutmeg
⅛	teaspoon sea salt
⅛	teaspoon ground cloves
6	pounds Granny Smith apples, cored, peeled and sliced ¼ inch thick

1. Melt butter in large skillet over medium heat. Stir in brown sugar, cinnamon, nutmeg, salt and cloves; mix well. Add apples; toss carefully in butter mixture to prevent apples from breaking up. Cook 5 minutes or until apples are tender.

2. Keep warm until served.

Makes 12 servings

Homemade Pumpkin Pie

PREP 20 minutes   **BAKE** 55 to 60 minutes

1   refrigerated prepared pie crust
    (½ of 15-ounce package)

2   tablespoons pumpkin pie spice

1   tablespoon sugar

½   teaspoon salt

3   large eggs, beaten

2½   teaspoons vanilla

1   can (15 ounces) solid-pack
    pumpkin

⅓   cup sour cream

1   can (14 ounces) sweetened
    condensed milk (NOT
    evaporated milk)

    Whipped cream (optional)

1. Preheat oven to 425°F. Roll pie crust into 11-inch circle on lightly floured surface. Press dough onto bottom and up sides of 9-inch deep-dish pie plate. Fold extra dough under and flute edges; set aside.

tip

Prepare pie a day ahead of time; cool as directed, then refrigerate overnight. Remove 1 hour before serving. Preheat oven to 250°F; heat pie 15 minutes.

2. Combine pie spice, sugar and salt in large bowl. Whisk in eggs and vanilla until smooth. Add pumpkin and sour cream; mix until smooth. Gradually mix in sweetened condensed milk; mix until well blended. Pour into prepared crust.

3. Bake 15 minutes at 425°F. Reduce oven temperature to 350°F. Continue baking 40 to 45 minutes or until knife inserted near center comes out clean. Cool on wire rack at least 1½ hours before serving. Top each piece with whipped cream, if desired.

Makes 8 servings

Apple Cranberry Streusel Pie

PREP 30 minutes   **BAKE** 1 hour

1 refrigerated prepared pie crust (½ of 15-ounce package)	**½ teaspoon ground cinnamon**
¾ cup all-purpose flour	**6 tablespoons butter, melted**
¾ cup plus 6 tablespoons packed light brown sugar, divided	**2 pounds Granny Smith apples, peeled and thinly sliced (5 cups)**
6 tablespoons uncooked old-fashioned oats	**1 can (about 16 ounces) whole-berry cranberry sauce**
	1½ tablespoons cornstarch

1. Preheat oven to 350°F. Roll pie crust into 12-inch circle on lightly floured work surface. Place in 9-inch pie pan; fold extra dough under and flute edge.

2. Combine flour, 6 tablespoons brown sugar, oats and cinnamon in medium bowl; mix well. Stir in butter until mixture is crumbly; set aside.

3. Place apples and cranberry sauce in large bowl. Combine remaining ¾ cup brown sugar and cornstarch in small bowl; mix well. Sprinkle over apples; toss gently until apples are evenly coated. Transfer to prepared pie crust. Sprinkle evenly with oat mixture.

4. Bake 1 hour or until apples are tender. Transfer to wire rack to cool. Serve warm.

Makes 8 servings

sweet finale

Southern Pecan Pie with Toffee Crunch

PREP 20 minutes   **BAKE** 40 to 45 minutes

- 1 **refrigerated prepared pie crust (½ of 15-ounce package)**
- 1¼ **cups dark corn syrup**
- 4 **eggs, lightly beaten**
- ¼ **cup (½ stick) butter, melted and cooled slightly**

- 2 **teaspoons vanilla**
- 1½ **cups pecan halves**
- 1 **cup toffee baking bits, divided**
- 1 **tablespoon all-purpose flour**

1. Preheat oven to 350°F. Roll pie crust into 12-inch circle on lightly floured work surface. Place in 9-inch pie pan; fold extra dough under and flute edge.

2. Combine corn syrup, eggs, butter and vanilla in medium bowl; mix well. Stir in pecans. Toss ⅔ cup baking bits with flour in small bowl; stir into pecan mixture. Pour into prepared crust.

3. Bake 40 to 45 minutes or until knife inserted in center comes out clean. Remove pie from oven; immediately sprinkle evenly with remaining baking bits. Cool completely on wire rack.

Makes 8 servings

sweet finale

Cake and Ice Cream "Pops"

PREP 25 minutes   **FREEZE** 50 minutes to 1 hour 10 minutes

1 **(10- to 12-ounce) pound cake**	**Multicolor sprinkles**
1 **pint ice cream, any flavor**	**Finely chopped nuts**
1½ **bottles (7¼ ounces each)**	**Crushed chocolate sandwich**
hard-coating chocolate topping	**cookies**
10 **mini forks or wooden picks**	**Chopped peppermint sticks**
	Toasted coconut

1. Line tray with plastic wrap. Remove pound cake from packaging. Slice ¼-inch thick piece from each end; reserve for another use. Cut remaining cake into ¾-inch thick slices. Cut circles with 1¾-inch diameter cookie cutter.

2. Place circles on prepared tray.

3. Top each cake circle with small scoop of ice cream, about 1¾-inch diameter.* Freeze 45 to 60 minutes or until ice cream is firm.

4. Pour chocolate topping into bowl. Remove prepared cake from freezer. Insert fork through ice cream into each piece of cake. Dip into chocolate topping to coat completely. Before coating dries, sprinkle with desired topping. Place pops on serving tray. Return to freezer 5 to 10 minutes or until coating is firm.

*A #20 ice cream scoop will make balls about 1¾ inches in diameter.

Makes 10 servings

tips

Coordinate the pops with any occasion. For example, use holiday flavors of ice cream such as pumpkin, cranberry or caramel to make the dessert festive throughout the fall and winter holidays, or decorate with seasonal candies for Valentine's Day or Easter.

Break leftover pieces of pound cake into small pieces and top with fresh fruit and whipped cream for a quick anytime dessert.